VAUDEVILLE

The Birth of
Show Business

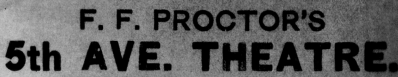

F. F. PROCTOR'S
5th AVE. THEATRE.

Broadway and Twenty-eighth Street.

CARRIAGE PARTIES RECEIVED AT THE 28th ST. ENTRANCE.

CONTINUOUS PERFORMANCE
......OF......
REFINED VAUDEVILLE
From Noon to 11 P. M.

On All Holidays Doors Open at 9.30 A. M.

PROGRAMME:
Fourth Week—Commencing Monday, May 28, 1900.

The various Artists do not necessarily appear in the order as given below.
See announcement cards at the side of the stage.

Vaudeville's Favorite Comedians,
THE FOUR COHANS,
In Geo. M. Cohans Latest Farcical Success,
"THE GOVERNOR'S SON"
CAST.

Benjamin Curtis, just Married and Jealous............ ....JERRY J. COHAN
Algy Wheelock, Only Son of Gov. Wheelock..... ....GEO. M. COHAN
Mrs. Dixon, the young bride, looking for her Runaway Husband
....JOSEPHINE COHAN

All the Musical numbers in this Farce written and composed by Geo. M. Cohan.

GEO. FULLER GOLDEN
THE FAVORITE MONOLOGUIST IN NEW SONGS AND SAYINGS.

ROSSOW MIDGETS
THE SMALLEST ATHLETES AND WRESTLERS IN THE WORLD.

Programme Continued on Second Page Following.

VAUDEVILLE

The Birth of Show Business

by Judy Alter

CrossRoads Middle School
Media Center

A FIRST BOOK

FRANKLIN WATTS
A Division of Grolier Publishing
New York • London • Hong Kong • Sydney
Danbury, Connecticut

~ 3 ~

Photographs ©:Archive Photos: 19, 31, 32, 34 right, 35, 41, 47 bottom, 51, 52, 56; Brown Brothers: cover, 2, 23, 26 bottom; CBS: 8 (Alan Singer); Corbis-Bettmann: cover, 12, 18, 24, 26 top, 37; Culver Pictures: 10, 11, 15, 17, 21, 30; Kobal Collection: 47 top, 54; New York Public Library Picture Collection: 22; Photofest: 27, 34 left, 36, 39, 40, 44, 46, 49.

Library of Congress Cataloging-in-Publication Data

Alter, Judy, 1938–
     Vaudeville: the birth of show business / by Judy Alter.
         p. cm. — (A First book)
     Includes bibliographical references and index.
     Summary: Discusses the history of vaudeville including performances, theaters, and actors, and examines its influence on modern entertainment.
     ISBN 0–531–20358–1
     1. Vaudeville—United States—History—Juvenile literature. [1. Vaudeville—History.] I. Title. II. Series.
PN1968.U5A38 1998
792.7'0973—dc21   97–44174
                                         CIP
                                         AC

CONTENTS

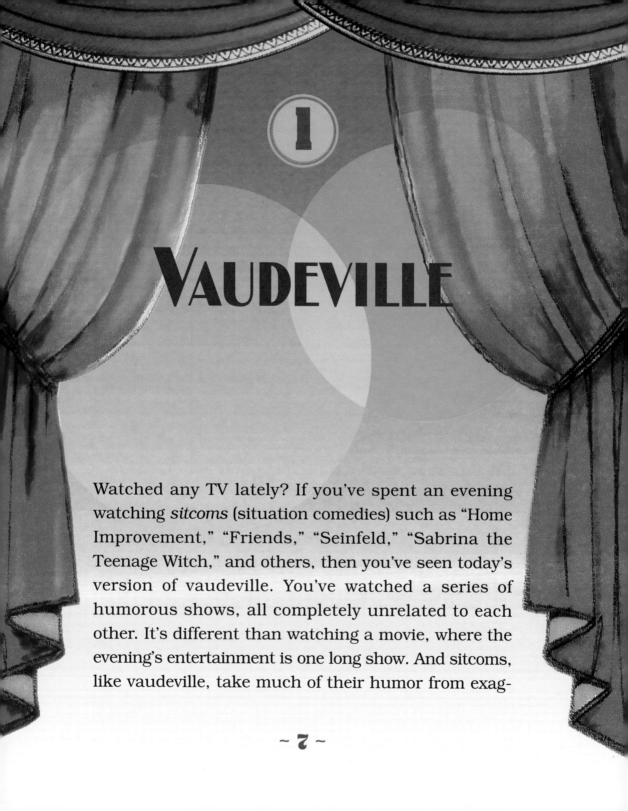

1

VAUDEVILLE

Watched any TV lately? If you've spent an evening watching *sitcoms* (situation comedies) such as "Home Improvement," "Friends," "Seinfeld," "Sabrina the Teenage Witch," and others, then you've seen today's version of vaudeville. You've watched a series of humorous shows, all completely unrelated to each other. It's different than watching a movie, where the evening's entertainment is one long show. And sitcoms, like vaudeville, take much of their humor from exag-

The Late Show *with David Letterman is one of today's versions of vaudeville entertainment.*

gerated or stereotyped characters—the nagging housewife, the husband who can do nothing right, the prim schoolteacher.

Maybe you've watched Jay Leno on *The Tonight Show* or David Letterman, the vaudeville comedians of the 1990s. They, too, present a series of unconnected acts. Or has your school had a talent show, with singing, dancing, and dramatic recitals? Then you've seen an example of vaudeville close to home.

Vaudeville is simply a series of entertaining acts that have little or no relation to each other but are presented in one performance. The acts are carefully chosen to provide the audience with a well-rounded evening of live entertainment. A typical vaudeville show during the early 1900s featured singing, dancing, juggling, magic, animal acts, comedians, and short dramatic scenes. The acts followed one another in rapid succession.

Vaudeville is a distinctly American form of entertainment. It was developed and refined in the United States in the nineteenth century. By the 1880s, vaudeville *troupes* toured the country, presenting bits of serious drama, concerts, operatic selections, ballet, musical comedy, and *pantomime*. For twenty or thirty years, traveling troupes would return to the same towns with the same acts. Eventually, the audiences knew every line, waited for every joke, and noticed every addition or change. From 1908 until 1935, the Avon Comedy 4 toured with an act called "The New Teacher," featuring four middle-aged men in a classroom. For almost twenty years they performed the act without changing a word or a gesture.

The Avon Comedy 4 presenting "The New Teacher"

Roots of Vaudeville

The roots of the name itself are not known for certain, but the term "vaudeville" may originate from two French phrases: *du Val de Vire*, which means "drinking songs," or *voix de ville*, which means "songs of the street." In this country, several people claimed to have coined the word "vaudeville." In 1871, Sargent's Great Vaudeville Company claimed to be the first to use "vaudeville."

Showman M. S. Leavitt, as well as John W. Ransone, also claimed to be the first.

Vaudeville may be traced back to minstrel singers in medieval Europe, to short comic acts performed between the parts of a serious play or opera, and even to *troubadours* who performed alone at European royal courts. However, vaudeville is most closely linked to the variety show.

VARIETY SHOWS

Variety shows were presented in saloons and beer halls during the mid-1800s. These shows tended to be heavy-handed, obvious, and frequently obscene. The jokes were crude, the humor was *slapstick*, and the actors relied on

John W. Ransone (left) was one of the first variety performers to use the term "vaudeville."

Most nineteenth-century beer halls were rowdy and vulgar; they were not considered places for respectable women or children. As a result, the early variety shows presented in these forums were usually seen by an audience made up almost entirely of men.

such obvious props as fright wigs and red noses to win laughs. Endless combinations of performers appeared on stage—singles, doubles, trios, quartets, *monologue* comedians, *ventriloquists* with wooden dummies, freak and odd acts, magicians, and big acts with fifteen or more performers. The vast majority of variety actors were male. Female characters were almost always played by men pretending to be women.

The heart of the variety show was comedy. Unfortunately, during the nineteenth century the comedy was often cruel. Many variety acts depended upon ridiculing or making fun of certain groups of people in ways that are now considered bigoted and sexist. The standard characters of a variety show included the dumb wife, the shrewish mother-in-law, the ugly girl-friend, the slow-witted black man, the stingy Jewish man, the German blockhead, and the Irish drunk. In portraying these characters, the vaudeville comedian used exaggerated accents and gestures to draw laughter from the audience. These shows drew upon popular stereotypes of certain groups of people and even made the stereotypes stronger.

The Minstrel Show

Perhaps the cruelest type of variety show was the minstrel show. These shows featured white actors who blackened their faces using burnt cork or greasepaint and wore striped trousers and straw hats. The actors performed racist imitations of black people, walking slowly and loosely around the stage and speaking in an uneducated manner. The main character was known as the "ignorant Negro" and demonstrated a slowness to understand and think. Today, blackface is denounced by civil rights organizations and is recognized as an insult to African-Americans. Blackface is rarely performed, even in historical presentations. From 1840 through 1880, however, minstrel shows were the most popular form of variety entertainment in the United States.

Many minstrel shows featured sentimental ballads, *soft-shoe dances*, and tunes played on the banjo (an instrument introduced by black folk music). The first minstrel show may have been performed by Thomas Daddy Rice in 1830. Rice toured the South playing songs he had learned from slaves on his family's plantation. His song, "Jump, Jim Crow," gave rise

Thomas Daddy Rice created the character known as Jim Crow. This character, which was based on offensive stereotypes of African-Americans, strengthened common prejudices against black people.

to the character of the "ignorant Negro" and may have given us the name for laws that discriminated against African-Americans after the Civil War. These laws, known as Jim Crow laws, were struck down by the Supreme Court in the 1960s.

MINSTREL TROUPES

Thomas Daddy Rice sang mainly in the South, where minstrel shows began. But these shows soon became popular in the North. Supposedly, the first minstrel act seen in New York was performed in 1843 by the Virginia Minstrels. The Kentucky Minstrels opened in New York that same year, followed by Christy's Minstrels in 1846.

E. P. Christy, the founder of Christy's Minstrels, commissioned composer Stephen C. Foster to write a song for his show. Foster, well known today for such southern songs as "Oh, Susanna" and "Camptown Races," was fascinated by the black music of the South. For Christy, he wrote "Swanee River," today a well-known traditional song. Foster was paid $500 for the song. Another classic song that was first performed by the Christy Minstrels is "Dixie," which was supposedly introduced by a blackface singer named Dan Emmett.

avoid paying their bills, and some cautious [...] ers put bars on their windows.

Before the Civil War, minstrel shows w[ere] operated, and performed by white people. Bu[t in the] 1860s, this began to change. By 1863, sev[e]ral minstrel shows were owned and operated by black people. One such show was the Ira Aldridge Troupe of Philadelphia, which was owned by a man who worked for the abolition of slavery. These troupes presented their traditional music, as it was played and sung on the Southern plantations, but they did not mimic the speech and body movements of former slaves. The troupe's audience was usually black and was generally unfriendly to white people who attended.

Ira Aldridge was one of several African-Americans to own a minstrel troupe after the Civil War. Aldridge was one of the first black Shakespearean actors to achieve world fame.

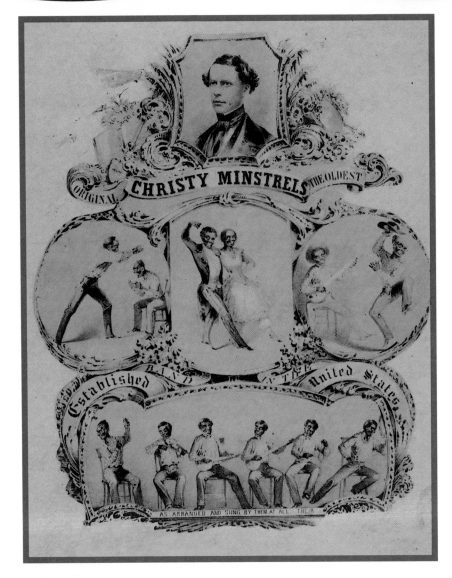

The Original Christy Minstrels was one of the most popular minstrel troupes.

Minstrel shows were big productions. Al Jo[lson]
from left, became one of vaudeville's bigge[st]

The entrance of a minstrel troupe in[to a town]
usually met with much excitement. Ty[pically, they]
arrived by train, sometimes with players h[anging off]
sides of the car. Their arrival meant a para[de and a cake-]
walk concert, for which the entire tow[n turned out.]
Sometimes, however, they left more quie[tly, especially]
if the profit from the show was not good[. Performers]
were occasionally known to sneak out a h[otel window.]

VAUDEVILLE'S GOLDEN ERA

Variety shows during the mid-1800s attracted audiences almost entirely made up of men. The rowdy beer-hall atmosphere, the obscene humor, and the *vulgar* sound effects were not considered appropriate for respectable women.

In the late 1880s, Tony Pastor of New York "cleaned up" the variety show in an effort to produce a show that would appeal to men and women and their families. Pastor had grown up performing in variety shows, doing blackface and song-and-dance acts. At fourteen he became the youngest circus ringmaster under a canvas tent, and at twenty-four he opened his first theater. Pastor himself starred as a singer and was known by fellow actors for hamming it up.

Tony Pastor is remembered for "cleaning up" the variety show and creating a form of entertainment suitable for families.

After a series of ventures in theater, some successful and some not, Pastor opened Tony Pastor's New Fourteenth Street Theater and presented a program of music and comedy sketches. His shows also featured acrobats who used tables, chairs, and brooms as props. Horseplay was not allowed, nor were off-color language or gestures. Traditional vaudeville was born. Pastor brought women—wives, sisters, and sweethearts—into the vaudeville audience. Frequently, whole families attended the shows. And he refined the show—no more *pratfalls* and vulgar noises.

By 1905 vaudeville had its own publication—the magazine *Variety*, which is still being published today.

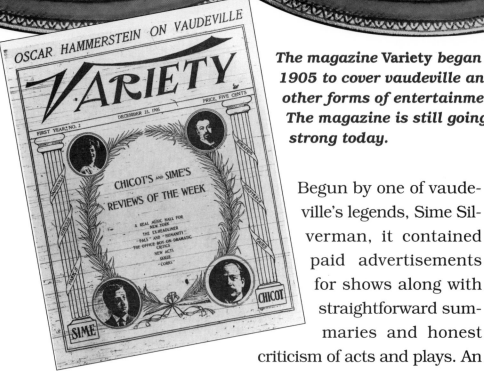

OSCAR HAMMERSTEIN ON VAUDEVILLE

VARIETY

PRICE, FIVE CENTS

FIRST YEAR; NO. 2   DECEMBER 23, 1905

CHICOT'S AND SIME'S
REVIEWS OF THE WEEK

A REAL MUSIC HALL FOR
NEW YORK
THE EX-HEADLINER
"PALS" AND "HUMANITY"
THE OFFICE-BOY-ON-DRAMATIC
CRITICS
NEW ACTS
SXIGIE
"CORKS"

SIME   CHICOT

The magazine Variety *began in 1905 to cover vaudeville and other forms of entertainment. The magazine is still going strong today.*

Begun by one of vaudeville's legends, Sime Silverman, it contained paid advertisements for shows along with straightforward summaries and honest criticism of acts and plays. An issue might contain a paid advertisement for a show—next to an unfavorable review of the same show. Today, *Variety* is still a powerful voice in the entertainment field.

THE PALACE

The first twenty years of this century were the golden era of vaudeville, although even then voices of gloom were predicting its early end. More than any other single theater, New York's Palace Theater made those twenty or more years golden. It was *the* vaudeville theater. The Palace, at the corner of 47th and Broadway,

The Palace

Vaudeville shows featured refined, usually comical, theatrical sketches.

was the dream of Martin Beck. As a teenager Beck had come to this country from Europe with a vaudeville troupe. After the troupe broke up, Beck continued in vaudeville and eventually ran what was called the Orpheum Circuit, a string of theaters between Chicago and California. But his dream was to have the best and biggest theater in New York, one that would show nothing but top-notch entertainment.

When the Palace opened in March 1913, rival theater owners gleefully predicted it would die a quick death. The acts for the first few weeks were well known to audiences of the day but not particularly remarkable, and crowds at the fancy crimson-and-gold theater were not as large as Beck had hoped. Then, in April, famed actress Ethel Barrymore played the Palace and things began to look up. But the player who really set the theater on its course for success was French dramatic actress Sarah Bernhardt. The Great Bernhardt was a legend in her own time, known for her dramatic power on stage and her unusual life offstage. It was rumored, for instance, that she preferred to sleep in a coffin. Whether it was the stories about her or her dramatic ability that drew audiences, people came by the hundreds, even though the price was increased for her show.

At the Palace, Bernhardt signed on for a two-week run and ended by playing almost four weeks. It was said she refused to play on the same bill with animal or blackface acts, and she demanded $500 in gold at the end of each performance.

(Other versions of the story say she accepted conventional money, but the truth seems to be that she was paid the unusually high sum of $1,000 a day for two performances.) Her appearance not only saved the Palace but also helped establish a higher standard for vaudeville shows. Bernhardt played the Palace several years later, when she was seventy years old and had lost a leg. The stage floor had to be covered with thick bear

Appearances at the Palace by renowned actresses Ethel Barrymore (top) and Sarah Bernhardt (bottom) helped make the theater a success soon after its opening.

This theater page from the March 25, 1913, edition of the New York Herald advertises many vaudeville shows including the opening of the Palace. An advertisement at the bottom left announces the first public appearance of Helen Keller in New York.

rugs to muffle the sound of her wooden leg, but for three weeks she held audiences spellbound with her portrayal of Joan of Arc.

Within five years of its opening, the Palace was the greatest variety theater in New York, offering "two-a-days" (two shows daily—a matinee or afternoon performance and an evening performance, usually offered seven days a week). It was the peak of achievement for a performer to play the Palace, but the theater catered to audiences so demanding that some stars—among them famed blackface singer Al Jolson—refused to play on its stage because they were afraid the audience might not be pleased and might not be polite about their displeasure. Performers at the Palace had to leave the audience gasping or crying for more.

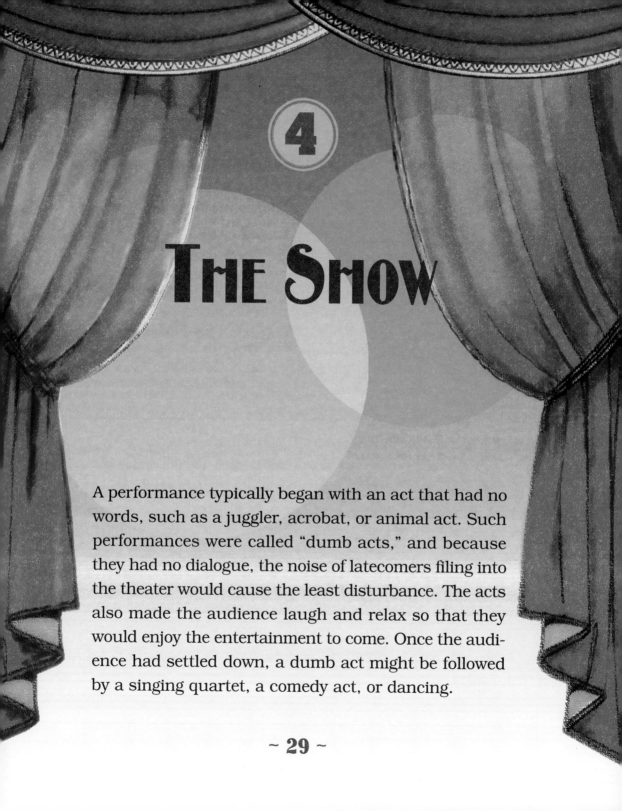

4

THE SHOW

A performance typically began with an act that had no words, such as a juggler, acrobat, or animal act. Such performances were called "dumb acts," and because they had no dialogue, the noise of latecomers filing into the theater would cause the least disturbance. The acts also made the audience laugh and relax so that they would enjoy the entertainment to come. Once the audience had settled down, a dumb act might be followed by a singing quartet, a comedy act, or dancing.

While vaudeville audiences filed into the theater, a show usually began with a "dumb act," an act without words that wouldn't be disrupted by the arriving crowd.

At the Palace, a new bill, or program, was presented weekly, usually with nine acts. New acts were first presented at Monday matinees, and large crowds of people paid $2 each to see the new acts try out. Many entertainers got their first "break," or chance, in show business at the Palace—Jack Benny played violin there, Ray Folger danced, comedienne Fanny

Brice did a burlesque of modern dance, and Sophie Tucker, the "Last of the Red Hot Mamas," appeared on stage. These names, unfamiliar now, were famous in their day and known to every American.

In classic vaude-ville, every performer was the boss of his or her own act—writer, producer, actor, and director. They worked hard at pleasing the audience, but only the

Sophie Tucker, a singer known a "The Last of the Red Hot Mamas," was a regular at the Palace. She is remembered for her brash, sassy style and her generosity to charitable organizations.

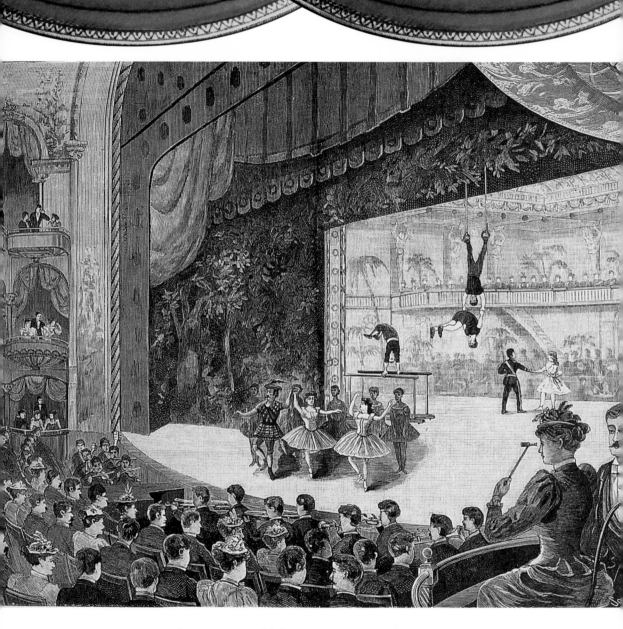

An opening act could have many performers.
The money they earned was split between them.

big stars made much money. In small shows, the pay ranged from $150 a week for an opening act to $450 for the star. An opening act often consisted of many performers—acrobats, balancers, tumblers, jugglers, comedians—and they had to split the money.

In a big traveling show or at the Palace, the salaries were better, especially for the star. The opening act was paid between $150 and $200 a week. The second act, generally a singing and dancing couple, might make $225 to $250. The star of the show could make as much as $750 to $1,500.

Performances were intimate—there were no microphones or other audio equipment between audience and actor. Singers sang loudly—*fortissimo*—and comedians projected their voices to the farthest upper balcony. Once when the audience complained they could not hear classic comedian Fred Allen beyond the fourth row, he walked off the stage and refused to return.

Vaudeville featured many talented black singers, dancers, and songwriters. By the early 1900s, there were nearly 300 black performers rated as principal or major actors, and a total of almost 1,500 in show business. Black musicians who began in vaudeville include Louis Armstrong, the Ink Spots, Sarah Vaughn,

Cab Calloway and Sarah Vaughn are two of the many African-American performers who began their careers in vaudeville.

Ethel Waters, Duke Ellington, and Cab Calloway. A black comedian remembered by old-timers is Eddie Anderson, who played Rochester on the *Jack Benny Program.*

VAUDEVILLE STARS

Al Jolson

From the 1910s through the 1940s, one of the most famous performers in America was a Jewish entertainer named Al Jolson. Jolson frequently sang in blackface and was best known for his rendition of "Mammy" and "Rock-a-Bye Your Baby." He was also a talented comedian and was known for taking many encores. He often announced an *encore* by telling the audience, "You ain't heard nothin' yet!" In private life, the successful entertainer was a bitterly unhappy man.

Al Jolson

Jolson was the son of a cantor (a traditional singer in the Jewish temple) who saw nothing to respect in his son's career. In 1927, Jolson increased his fame by starring in the first "talking" movie, *The Jazz Singer*. The movie, which was remade in the 1980s, is based on Jolson's own life.

Will Rogers

Will Rogers would twirl a lasso while delivering a comic monologue.

Will Rogers was a very different type of vaudeville performer. Part Cherokee Indian, he grew up on an Oklahoma ranch, where he learned to use a lasso. He became so good at throwing a rope that he started working in Wild West shows. Rogers soon took his lasso act to the vaudeville stage. During his lasso performances, he began making humorous remarks about political and current events, twirling a rope the whole time. His simple, straightforward, but clever humor quickly made him a vaudeville star.

After playing on the vaudeville stage, Rogers starred in movies, wrote six books, and became the friend of presidents, senators, and kings. He died at the height of his career in a 1935 plane crash in Alaska. Rogers is remembered for one of his most famous sayings: "I never met a man I didn't like."

Fanny Brice

Fanny Brice, one of the greatest singing comediennes in the history of American theater, sang both comedic and tragic songs. For comedy, she had the advantage of a funny face with large eyes and an unusual smile. She worked her Jewish heritage into her comedy routines, sprinkling in Yiddish terms, pretending not to understand

Fanny Brice was known for her expressive face.

English, and presenting Jewish impersonations—often a boasting Yiddish mother or a hat shop salesgirl. Always ambitious to entertain, Brice began singing onstage as a child. By 1910, she was performing in *The Ziegfeld Follies*, a famous New York revue, and the pace of her career never slowed down. She sang at the Palace, played in movies, and became a popular radio personality as "Baby Snooks." She is also remembered for saying, "I've been rich, and I've been poor. Rich is better!" Her life story has been told in books and on the stage several times. The best-known version is the play *Funny Girl*, which was later made into a movie starring Barbra Striesand.

Bill "Bojangles" Robinson

Bill "Bojangles" Robinson was a black vaudevillian who began singing and dancing onstage at the age of six. For years he toured the South with black companies, but he was fifty years old before he ever danced for a white audience. Robinson changed the nature of tap dancing by dancing on his toes, and he performed a "stair dance" in which his feet seemed to be climbing an imaginary set of stairs. He was also famous for running backwards—he set a world record of 8.2 seconds for the 75-yard backwards dash—and for eating ice cream by the quart. Have you ever heard anyone say "copasetic," meaning "OK"? Robinson made this word part of our daily speech. He became known for wearing a plaid suit and for always smiling while dancing in a *revue* titled *Blackbirds of 1928.* His nickname, "Bojangles," meant happy-go-lucky to white people and "squabbler" to black people. After vaudeville disappeared, Bojangles played in fourteen movies and several stage shows.

Bill "Bojangles" Robinson's plaid suit became one of his trademarks.

Nora Bayes

Singer Nora Bayes was billed as "The Greatest Single Woman Singing Comedienne in the World." She wore outrageous outfits—sequined dresses and large hats of peacock feathers—and traveled in a private railroad car with servants to take care of her. When she shared the stage with her husband, Jack Norworth, she insisted on the billing, "NORA BAYES, Assisted and Admired by Jack Norworth." She began her vaudeville appearances around 1900, and by 1907 she was appearing in New York's Fifth Avenue Theatre. From there she went on to *The Ziegfeld Follies*, which she left because she claimed that Florenz Ziegfeld, the show's founder and producer, wanted her to wear tights and ride a pink elephant. By 1916, Bayes was singing at the Palace, and by 1921 she was one of the stars who earned big money ($3,500 a week). She became increasingly difficult to work with, however, and was soon banned from the Palace. Her temper, probably a sign of ill health, got her in trouble in other theaters too. Her last stage appearance was

Nora Bayes

in 1928, just before she died of cancer. She is remembered for such songs as "Over There," "Has Anybody Seen Kelly?," and "Shine on, Harvest Moon."

The Marx Brothers

Not all vaudeville stars worked alone. One of the best known groups was the Marx Brothers—Groucho, Harpo, Chico, Gummo, and Zeppo. Groucho was the

The Marx Brothers with their father (left to right: father, Harpo, Groucho, Chico, Zeppo)

first to go on stage, singing in a trio in 1905 at the age of ten. His brother Gummo joined him and, with two nonfamily members, they called themselves the Four Nightingales. But the Marx Brothers' strength lay in comedy, not music. In 1912 their uncle, Al Shean, wrote a sketch titled "Fun in Hi Skool" for Groucho, Gummo, Harpo, and Chico. Groucho played the schoolteacher trying to teach three outrageously dumb pupils. In 1914, Shean wrote them another sketch, "Home Again," which they played until World War I, when Gummo was drafted and replaced in the act by the fifth brother, Zeppo. (All the brothers tried to volunteer, but the others were rejected for various physical reasons.) The Marx Brothers first played the Palace in 1915, and throughout the 1920s they were the headline act. The act fell apart when the brothers wanted the respect given to Broadway stars (but not to vaudeville comedians). They went their separate ways, playing in Broadway shows and countless movies. Groucho was the best known and the easiest to recognize by his bushy, dark eyebrows and thick, black mustache.

5

THE DECLINE OF TRADITIONAL VAUDEVILLE

In the late 1920s, attendance at the Palace dropped off. The "Roaring Twenties" was an era of unusual entertainment—flagpole sitting, rocking-chair contests, and dance marathons—and people were attracted to these outdoor events. But most of all, radio and silent movies drew audiences away from vaudeville. By the time movies with dialogue began appearing in the late twenties, vaudeville was in rapid decline.

Radio Shows

With the rise of radio shows, former vaudeville fans could lie on the couch at home and listen to their favorite entertainers on radio. The sense of closeness found in the theater was lacking, and sometimes an act that was fascinating on stage lost some of its charm through microphones and radio transmission. Never-

As vaudeville began to decline, Gracie Allen and George Burns became favorites on radio and then on television and in movies.

theless, radio shows enjoyed a rapid rise in popularity throughout the 1920s and 1930s. Fanny Brice found fame as "Baby Snooks" on radio, and George Burns and Gracie Allen were longtime radio favorites. Fibber McGee and Mollie were another favorite couple, and the sound of things crashing out of Fibber McGee's cluttered closet became familiar to thousands of Americans. Today, many older people still refer to an overcrowded closet as "Fibber McGee's closet."

MOTION PICTURES

Dramatic silent films began appearing in the United States in the early 1900s. *The Great Train Robbery*, an eleven-minute silent Western released in 1903, was the first of its kind. By the mid-1910s, silent films had come into their own, and during the 1920s they began to compete seriously with vaudeville for audiences. Charlie Chaplin became a superstar of silent comedies, and William S. Hart and Douglas Fairbanks were stars of silent action films.

In 1927, vaudeville great Al Jolson starred in *The Jazz Singer*, the first movie with dialogue. These new movies with sound, called "talkies," quickly became popular, and vaudeville could not keep up. The last traditional vaudeville show at the Palace played in 1932.

*In 1927, **The Jazz Singer** brought dialogue to the big screen.*

Then the theater began to show motion pictures. For several years, like many early movie houses, the Palace mixed vaudeville acts with moving pictures. In fact, many early moving pictures simply presented vaudeville acts on screen instead of stage. At many points in these movies, the actors would break into vaudeville dance performances that related very little to the story

A still from The Great Train Robbery, *the first major silent film*

Charlie Chaplin movies and other silent films began to compete with vaudeville for audiences in the 1920s.

being told. These elaborately designed dance numbers were typical of movies well into the 1940s.

Vaudeville itself was partly to blame for its own disappearance. New theaters, such as Radio City Music Hall in New York, presented elaborate dance and symphony numbers, drawing crowds from the vaudeville theaters. As attendance declined, vaudeville producers lowered the salaries of the performers and the quality of the shows. In one theater, "two-a-days" were replaced with five shows a day. No performer could give his best five times a day, seven days a week, and remain fresh for the audience.

VAUDEVILLE'S REVIVAL

In the 1950s, the Palace saw a revival of vaudeville. Two-a-day variety acts were combined with first-run movies. Beginning in October 1951, singer Judy Garland (best known now for her role in *The Wizard of Oz)* performed in the Palace's vaudeville revival, and audiences flocked to the theater. First signed to sing for four weeks, Garland stayed for nineteen. She opened her act by telling audiences, "Since I was a kid the one thing I've dreamed of was playing the Palace."

Even after Garland left, the Palace's revival ran for seven years, showing about 300 eight-act shows.

Old acts from vaudeville were brought back, and new acts appeared as well. Opera star Lauritz Melchior appeared in a comedy act, and gravel-voiced Jimmy Durante sang with opera star Helen Traubel. Most of the other names who appeared are long forgotten, unfamiliar to us today.

The revival eventually ran out of steam. Although some hoped the Palace would continue to offer a stage for stars of old vaudeville, the truth was that by the early 1960s there were not enough vaudeville actors around to fill a show. Many had moved on to television and movies, some had grown too old to work, and some had died.

Judy Garland (front, in dark coat) poses with the cast of the Palace's vaudeville revival in 1952.

VAUDEVILLE'S LEGACY

Today, traditional vaudeville is gone. Vaudeville has, however, strongly influenced current forms of entertainment. During the decline of vaudeville, many performers retired from show business. But many others started new careers in radio and movies—the same industries that had contributed to vaudeville's demise. Eventually, television provided another forum for former vaudeville performers to entertain the public.

TELEVISION

Traditional vaudeville was a thing of the past by the time televisions became common fixtures in most homes. In a sense, though, the small television screen brought vaudeville-like entertainment to more people than the Palace, or any other vaudeville theater, ever

In the late 1940s and early 1950s, television began to replace radio as the primary form of family entertainment. Many performers who began in vaudeville became popular television personalities.

The Ed Sullivan Show *mimicked the vaudeville format by presenting a series of short, unrelated acts. The show introduced the Beatles (pictured here with Ed Sullivan) to American audiences in 1964.*

had. With television, every home became a vaudeville theater and every watcher was his own critic. Like a vaudeville audience, the television audience had a pro-gram—from their daily newspaper—that told them what act or show was coming next.

Many television shows imitate vaudeville's for-mat of presenting many unrelated acts. This variety format was especially widespread in the early days of television. *The Ed Sullivan Show*, a popular program that ran from 1948 to 1971, introduced American audiences to many talented performers who went on to fame and fortune, including the Beatles and Elvis Presley. For many years, television also kept some of vaudeville's most important performers before the public eye. George Burns, Jack Benny, Jimmy "The Nose" Durante, Bob Hope, Milton Berle, Lucille Ball, and many others appeared frequently on the small screen. Dancers such as Fred Astaire and Ray Bolger were popular on television, as was Danny Kaye, who often incorporated dance routines into his comedy acts.

THE LAST OF THE VAUDEVILLIANS

In 1996, George Burns died at the age of 100, and Bob Hope, then ninety-three, presented his last television special. Both events were significant for fans of vaudeville, for Burns and Hope were the last two performers from vaudeville's golden age. And they are two of the few names from vaudeville that are familiar to later generations that know little or nothing of the great stars of the vaudeville era.

George Burns had been onstage, one way or another, since 1903. As a teenager in vaudeville, he

While in his late seventies, George Burns earned an Academy Award for his performance in the 1975 film **The Sunshine Boys***. Pictured above, Burns (seated) costarred with Walter Matthau.*

did everything from trick roller-skating to performing with a trained seal. Whatever act the producer wanted, he once said, just happened to be his specialty. In 1923 he met Gracie Allen, a red-haired Irish comedienne, and they teamed up. Three years later they were married. In their act, George played Gracie's patient husband, always slightly amused by her scatterbrained antics. "Oh, George, I bet you say that to all the girls!" was Gracie's trademark line. George always closed the show with the line, "Say goodnight, Gracie," to which she'd respond, "Goodnight Gracie."

George and Gracie were most successful on the radio, but they also had an eight-year show on TV that was a combination of vaudeville and situation comedy, with George acting as narrator. Gracie died in 1964 of heart disease, and though George never remarried, he did rebuild his career as a single actor. In 1975 he won an Oscar for Best Supporting Actor, playing an aging vaudeville performer in *The Sunshine Boys*. At the age of eighty-one, George played the role of God in the movie *Oh God!* and its sequel. Burns said this about the role: "Why shouldn't I play God? Anything I do at my age is a miracle." Burns, who made his old age a part of his comic routine, frequently played big casinos in Las Vegas. He scheduled shows in London and Las Vegas for his 100th birthday, but a fall in 1994 seriously injured him, and he was unable to keep those dates.

Bob Hope began his career on the vaudeville stage in the 1920s. By the mid-1930s, he was on radio; then came movies and television. Hope achieved

Early in his career, a young Bob Hope (right) poses with his vaudeville partner Lloyd Durbin.

stardom in motion pictures, appearing with such movie stars as Dorothy Lamour and Bing Crosby. In later years he became known for the Christmas specials he performed overseas for those serving in the United States armed forces. Bob Hope, a friend of presidents from Franklin Roosevelt to Bill Clinton, has never been afraid to turn his razor-sharp wit on the famous and powerful.

With George Burns gone and Bob Hope retired, traditional vaudeville and the last of its stars have departed the entertainment world. The variety-show format is less popular on television today, although such shows as *The Tonight Show* do occasionally present monologues by *stand-up comedians*, singing acts, and the like. But the basic elements of vaudeville survive in our television entertainment. Comedy is the mainstay of many week-night shows. Beavis and Butthead perform a modernized version of the dueling dialogue that used to take place between Lum 'n Abner (two black comedians of vaudeville and early radio). Rosie O'Donnell and Whoopi Goldberg fill the comedienne roles once played by such women as Fanny Brice.

Some old-time performers may moan that vaudeville is a lost art, and the vaudeville of the 1910s is indeed unlikely to be revived. But the spirit of vaudeville persists in modern entertainment, changing to meet the nature and needs of our culture.

GLOSSARY

encore — again or once more; in theater, a number or song presented after the end of the show in response to applause; an addition to the program

monologue — a tale told by a single speaker; entertainment by a single speaker

pantomime — an entire play or act in which the characters express themselves with gestures and bodily movements instead of dialogue

pratfall — a deliberate fall in which the falling person lands on the seat of his pants

revue — a theatrical presentation consisting of short, loosely connected songs, dances, and dramatic sketches

sitcoms (situation comedies) — on television, comedies in which the same characters appear in the same situation week after week, and the comedy comes from their situation; examples would be "Seinfeld," "Home Improvement," "Friends," and many others

slapstick — comedy characterized by wild action, such as throwing a pie in the actor's face; horseplay

soft-shoe dances — tap dances done without taps on the shoes; the result is a sort of shuffling sound

stand-up comedian — a comedian who delivers a comic speech while all alone on the stage

troubadour — a wandering singer (in Europe, principally in France, in the Middle Ages)

troupe — a group of singers, actors, or performers who travel together

ventriloquist — one who can speak with little or no movement of the lips so that the speech appears to come from somewhere or someone else—in this case, from a dummy or a doll; the ventriloquist also controls the movements of the dummy while seeming completely detached

vulgar — not showing good manners or taste; crude, coarse, unrefined; off-color

FOR MORE INFORMATION

BOOKS

Barr, Roger. *Radios: Wireless Sound.* San Diego: Lucent Books, 1994.

Bennett, Cathereen L. *Will Rogers: Quotable Cowboy.* Minneapolis: Runestone Press, 1995.

Brown, Pam. *Charlie Chaplin: Comic Genius Who Brought Laughter and Hope to Millions.* Milwaukee: G. Stevens Children's Books, 1991.

Diamond, Arthur. *Charlie Chaplin.* San Diego: Lucent Books, 1995.

Platt, Richard. *Film.* New York: Knopf, 1992.

Riehecky, Janet. *Television.* Tarrytown, N.Y.: Benchmark Books, 1996.

Tyson, Peter. *Groucho Marx.* New York: Chelsea House Publishers, 1994.

INTERNET RESOURCES

The American Variety Stage: Vaudeville and Popular Entertainment, 1870–1920

http://lcweb2.loc.gov/ammem/vshtml/vshome.html

At this site, the Library of Congress presents a collection of photographs, playbills, scripts, motion pictures, and sound recordings from the vaudeville era.

The Official Al Jolson Page

http://www2.ari.net/ajr/recs/

This site features lots of information, including pictures and sound clips, about this popular vaudeville entertainer.

The Roaring 1920s Concert Extravaganza

http://bestwebs.com/roaring1920/index.html

This site features recordings of famous vaudeville performers such as Fanny Brice and Al Jolson.

Vintage Vaudeville and Ragtime Show

http://www.bestwebs.com/vaudeville/

This virtual vaudeville show at the Palace features old sound clips of famous songs and routines and pictures of popular performers. The songs and monologues come from rare turn-of-the-century recordings.

INDEX

ABOUT THE AUTHOR

Judy Alter is the author of many novels and several dozen books for children, including Franklin Watts First Books *Rodeos: The Greatest Show on Dirt; Beauty Pageants: Tiaras, Roses, and Runways; The Comanches*; and *Women of the Old West.* She is the director of Texas Christian University Press, which publishes literature and history of Texas and the American West. She also holds a Ph.D. in English from Texas Christian University. Dr. Alter lives in Fort Worth, Texas.